Introduction

Colleen and Shirley met because they each had a friend who were friends. Colleen's friend Kathryn has known Shirley's friend Lindsay since childhood because their mothers were good friends.

Colleen channels Angels and has learned a lot from her very powerful Guardian Angel Zeduo (Zay-dwah). Channeling is a unique God-given gift. Colleen feels the presence of Angels and Spirits as they channel through her.

Shirley was able to record, transcribe and edit the many stories and teachings that Zeduo chose to share. Shirley's loving Guardian Angel Celia helped guide her through the process of composing this book.

This book is composed of channeled information that Zeduo would like to share with you. We hope his words resonate with your Spirit, and your Guardian Angel guides you on your Path to finish your Journey so that you can fulfill your Mission here on earth.

This book evolved through many conversations with Colleen's Guardian Angel Zeduo. The words in this book are from Zeduo ~ which were sorted, combined and edited to create the following chapters under his guidance.

What happens when I pray?

When you pray, you're asking for help. You have a problem and you're asking for someone to help. You or somebody else, like a family member or neighbor, has a problem going on and you want what's best for them, so you pray. When you pray, it puts you in a frame of mind. Everyone who prays or asks for help or seeks guidance through meditation, is calling upon someone who is not of this world for help. Human beings are all praying to a higher being regardless of what they call their deity. Many names are given to this deity. Colleen calls her deity "God" and we will refer to the higher being in this book as "God".

When you pray ~ your Guardian Angel hears you. God's gift to each of us is a Guardian Angel. Angels are his favored, most loved beings. Your Guardian Angel is your specific assistant ~ one who loves you very much and wants nothing but what's best for you. When you pray and you're asking for help, the power of prayer comes from within you. The more you pray, the more connected you get to your Guardian Angel. Even if you're asking for someone else, you are connecting more with your Guardian Angel.

The more you pray, the more the power comes from within you.

Angels are as different as humans ~ in personality, likes and dislikes. With respect to Shirley's family, their Guardian Angels have a very close-knit relationship. When Shirley prays for her children's happiness and safety, her Guardian Angel Celia passes this on to their Guardian Angels. Their Guardian Angel will say: "He needs love now" or "She needs support now" and Celia will go and give them a hug and they feel that closeness. The children know in their hearts that you're thinking of them right then and there, even though you're not there at the moment. Celia was withholding the help until they really needed it the most and then they get a whole big shot of love or a shot of confidence that they really needed at that time.

The Angels listen really well when you go to the heart of things and pray effectively. It is important to pray with the bigger picture of life in mind ~ what's for your best and highest good. There are people out there who pray for small simple things like a new dress or senseless things like wanting to be a

millionaire, and they're upset when God doesn't give them that. If it's not on their Path to have that, then that won't happen. Maybe praying for a new dress could be for your "best and highest good", but if that dress isn't important in the "bigger picture", then it won't happen. It's good to pray for small, simpler things but if you don't get them, you should realize you weren't suppose to have them. When you pray for bigger things and they come to pass, you'll know your prayers were answered. If they don't happen, you can amend your prayers to ask either for you to accept the reality of your life or pray for someone else or something else to change for the better.

Praying is asking for a being other than yourselves to help you either spiritually, physically, emotionally or mentally. Humans are made up of four basic things: you are a spiritual being, you are a physical being, you are an emotional being and you are a mental being. You are all four things and none of these four by itself should define you. If you're praying for yourself, or maybe someone else is sick, or maybe you have something coming up ~ when you pray ~ your Guardian Angel hears your prayers and

may field it to another Angel. God hears all prayers but he has Angels who take care of them for him.

Maybe you're having questions or doubts about things on the spiritual end, for example: "Is there a God?" "Why did God do this to me?" "I've got too much on my plate and God should take some of this away!" Those are all spiritual questions and your Guardian Angel will help you by keeping it simple, soothing you with peaceful thoughts and filling you with love. In your heart you always know the answers to the questions ~ everybody does ~ but sometimes it's just hard because there's so much going on that "you can't see the forest through the trees" on the spiritual end.

When you pray, it is usually your Guardian Angel who helps you, but other Angels may also field your prayers. If there's something that your Guardian Angel can't do for you, then he or she may field it to an Archangel. Archangels are leaders within the Angel community. All Guardian Angels will field prayers to Archangels and they do what they can to help out, and that's just your Angel "asking for help".

Archangel Gabriela is head of all the Angels. She helps choose your Guardian Angel when you are at the Light based on what your Path will be and the experiences your Spirit wants to encounter. Archangel Raphael is our "healer" and may be called upon to help with physical problems. Archangel Michael may be able to help you with large problems and is a champion at fighting really negative things. Archangel Arial is our "health and wellness" Angel and would help address issues that you personally have going on in your body.

You have to remember that when you're praying for somebody, you pray for what's their "best and highest good". And their "best and highest good" may not be the result that you think you are praying for. Their "best and highest good" would always be to stay on their Path and finish their Journey so that they can fulfill their Mission.

What is a Guardian Angel?

Angels are loving beings whom God created. An Angel is a beam of light and all Angels are made of light and love. Angels don't have a body but we have free will, which God gave us along with everybody else. Since the beginning, when God created us, he wanted light beings of love ~ he wanted beings around him who loved. Angels have been around billions and billions of years ~ billions of years before Earth or any of the Heavens were created and almost all of us were created at the same time within your Solar System.

Angels help each other along the way and we have what you would call an extended family because all Angels are connected. I'm in the dimension that we call the "Light" and Colleen calls it "Heaven". Even though, I ~ Zeduo ~ am talking to you right now, I'm not on earth right now; I'm not sitting next to you right now. Colleen is channeling me and I am talking through Colleen while she is sitting next to you. We don't have the five senses like you have, we can't smell, taste or see things like your human eyes do. However, we can certainly love and feel

disappointment. Our love for each other and all of God's beings is immeasurable.

God's gift to each human being is a Guardian Angel. When a Guardian Angel is assigned a human being, we call them our "charge". Colleen is Zeduo's charge and Shirley is Celia's charge. There are millions more human beings than Angels at any given time on earth and because of that, we have to multi-task. We can have several of you at one time. Celia could have 40, 50, 60 other charges ~ other human beings all around the earth. Your Guardian Angel is your personal assistant ~ one who loves you very much and wants nothing but what's best for you. Your Guardian Angel takes care of you and guides you.

Your Guardian Angel lives in your heart and in order to be in contact with your Guardian Angel, you need to *listen to your heart*. In order for you to listen to your Angel you must quiet your mind, quiet your life and listen with your heart for that is where your Angel lives. If a charge is going off their Path or if they are doing something that they are not supposed to do or if they should be doing something else ~ your Guardian Angel will try to show you. They may show you

through dreams or feelings, for instance, if a decision is good or not. Believe in and trust your Guardian Angel and you will never look back because you will be on your Path fulfilling your Mission.

Angels can tell you if you're on your Path. We can answer questions like: "Is this a good time to move to a new city?" "Is it a good time to change jobs?" "Is it a good time to separate from my husband?" "Should I accept this new opportunity?" Your Guardian Angel can tell you if that is on your Path and if today is a good time to do that. And a lot of times the timing might not be right and you may need to look into that in the future. You may need to look into another job or you may need to look into what your life would be like without your partner or you may need to look into moving out of town, away from family and friends.

If it's on your Path and you go with the flow, you're going to get there, but maybe not in your time frame. Let's say you hate your job, you don't like the people there and you don't like the drive back and forth. You don't like any of it but it's just not a good time for you to move right now and you know that. You may be

unhappy and perhaps are suffering in silence. A lot of people do that because they're afraid to say anything that might jeopardize their job because they need that income. If you get a chance to talk to someone like Colleen who is able to talk to your Angel and your Angel says: "This is where you need to be right now" ~ you can then turn your whole thinking around and say, "Ok, I have to be here and so I might as well make the best of it". If it's on your Path to stay, then there is reason for that and you will continue to fulfill your Mission. It could be to meet a person who is important for your future while still at the same job or to learn more about something that will allow you to move on to a more fulfilling position.

When you ask for guidance but don't follow the guidance, it's much better not to ask. Unfortunately, it can create a domino effect because if you ask for guidance and you don't take it, then certain things start happening to you that shouldn't happen to you. Sickness can crop up out of nowhere, loss of job, loss of friends, riffs with family members, not sleeping night after night. And as much as you didn't want to do something, then tomorrow it's twice as hard

as it was and then four times as hard as it was and
then your life starts going downhill until you can
get yourself to accept that the original guidance is
what you need to do. It's your own mind ~ not your
Angel's ~ that is causing the downhill spiral, because
you are off your own Path. It's easier to do something
from the beginning ~ to make a change ~ but if you
don't make a change, then it keeps getting harder and
harder to turn yourself around.

Don't resist your Path. For instance, if surgery is on
your Path, then, to start complaining about the pain
the second you come out of the operation will only
slow up your recovery time. It can even stop your
recovery or you might not recover right and you won't
properly heal your body because you're so negative
and pushing against what was meant to be. Or you
can say: "You know what, it's uncomfortable because
of the pain, but I have to do this in order to better
myself in the future". You certainly want to be here
a long time, for years and years and so why not be in
the best health you can be, and sometimes that means
you may need to have repairs done to your body. Just
go with the flow ~ settle down and realize that this is

it until your period of confinement is over with and then you can start back on your routine of living.

Your Guardian Angel lives in your heart, and the more you are able to listen to your heart ~ the more you will feel your Angel's guidance. Your Guardian Angel loves you very much and wants nothing but what's for your best and highest good, while guiding you on your Path to fulfill your Mission.

What are Spirits?

"Spirits" are beings at the "Light" and God gives them the chance to come down to earth so they can grow through human experiences. All human beings are Spirits. Many people call "Spirits"~ "Souls". Spirits and Souls are the same thing. We call our home the "Light" because everybody there is a light being. Colleen calls it "Heaven". We are all of the light and God is the brightest light of all of us ~ the creator of all. Spirits don't have a body ~ it's just energy. The more advanced your Spirit is, the more light will be given off. As you encounter the light of another Spirit, you sense an energy. Spirits recognize each other from past lives, whether you were together in 600 B.C. or 1412 A.D. There's a knowingness there but it's all energy based.

When you pass, you have a picture in your mind of people whom you knew and you carry that along with you. Let's say you live 30 more years than your Dad did ~ your Dad's not going to age 30 more years in your eyes. However, Spirits don't always think of themselves as looking like what they did when they passed ~ being young or old, tall or short, or having certain facial features ~ none of that. And since

they remember all their past lives, they might take a life image that was four lifetimes ago because that was pleasing to them. Others don't see themselves as other Spirits do or see other Spirits as they see themselves, but you do recognize each other through energy.

Spirits can have different experiences on earth than what they can have at the Light: the earth is like a school for Spirits. Spirits have the opportunity to grow on earth ~ to be able to explore and see just how far they can evolve. On earth, Spirits can experiment with the senses because in the Light you have emotions ~ love, happiness, disappointment ~ but on earth you can also smell, taste, feel and see beautiful landscapes. You can experiment with types of foods ~ different spices ~ that kind of thing. You also have the choice to smell different flowers, go different places and see different things ~ mountains, deserts, green trees, lush valleys and take in all these things. When you're at the Light you can't experiment with the senses ~ so you can't grow that way.

After a lifetime, some Spirits might wait 2,000 years to come back down to earth again as a human being

and others may come back the next year. Many Spirits at the Light are afraid to come to earth ~ and for good reasons. They may have suffered great harm on earth. It could very well have been that their life was taken before they had a chance to finish their Path and their Journey was cut short last time on earth. They really want to come back, but they're afraid to. No one else is pulling them back, they are the ones doing that because they are afraid to get out there and experiment again.

How quickly you learn on earth depends on how much you put yourself out there. You put yourself out there by helping people out, because this is what being human is all about. Many children are taught not to put themselves out there. For instance, in affluent countries such as the United States, you're taught at a very young age that you don't talk to certain kids. "She's dirty or she doesn't have a $90 dress like you, so don't talk to her because she's beneath you". Very strong Spirits will break away from that and say: "She looked like she needed a friend and I just went over and said Hi to her". That's how you progress faster, faster, faster ~ you take yourself out of the equation

and you just think of other people and you just help
them. Whatever they need ~ even if it's no more
than a smile or a "Hi!" or "Isn't this a great day?"
~ just to lift somebody's spirits. And there are so
many people who won't do that and there are millions
of people who need it ~ to hear somebody ~ anybody
~ speak to them. "They looked at me, they talked
to me and that's what I needed". *Helping others is
a gift to yourself!*

Some Spirits come down to taste food, feel romance,
smell flowers ~ especially those of you that have been
on earth many many times. The experienced Spirits
miss the human senses because those memories stay
with the Spirit. However, when you come down to
earth for a human lifetime, you don't remember your
past lives. You don't remember where you lived,
you don't remember what the food tasted like in the
regions that you lived because most likely you're not
of the same ethnic background in this life as you have
been in past lives. You could have been on another
continent and ate different foods that aren't even
available in your present life; different spices, different
meats and different preparations of things. Because

you don't remember, you can't remember some of the things that in your past life you used to eat and loved because now you're experiencing new things that you like. Once you pass and go back into the Light, all of those memories will flood back into the memory banks of your Spirit, and then you can compare. "Well I kind of liked this fish better than that fish", because now you've eaten several types of fish and many different preparations of fish and you can compare them now. And I'm using food as an example, because most everybody can taste.

You don't have the ability to remember your past lives, your past mistakes, past likes, past dislikes ~ but you can certainly recognize people. Not everybody does, but some can just look at a crowd and a face jumps out. You just know that you recognize that person even though you haven't met that person before in this lifetime and you might not ever see them again.

There are certain people in your life who come to you at very specific times in your life. If they would have come to you at other times in your life, you wouldn't have had a relationship with them at all. For example,

Shirley and Colleen's relationship in collaborating
on this book together. Shirley met Colleen at a
time in her life where she was reading a lot about
spirituality and they happened to be at the same party
and happened to meet and happened to strike up a
conversation. There were quite a few people at the
party and it could very well have been that the two
women may never have had a opportunity to talk.
You could say that it was their Paths that brought
Shirley and Colleen together.

*When you are on earth, you are all human beings. You
should always keep this in mind and act like human
beings. Love yourself, help others and be tolerant,
patient and loving.*

What is a Path?

A Path is a goal that you choose at the Light and you stick with it through thick and thin, when times are hard, when times are good. You sit down with an Angel and figure out what you want to accomplish in life. At the Light you can see and understand what is happening on earth, all at the same time. You have one main goal on your Path and it is about something that is happening on the earth right now. It's about broad, huge, and even awful things going on. Huge injustices ~ like bullying, hunger, war, intolerance, corruption. Your goal always has something to do with accomplishing good within the "Big Picture" of things.

If you come down to earth to stop war, then that is the main goal of your Path and you need to be a peace advocate. You will come into a family where the people will be an advantage to you in achieving your goal. For example, say that you chose to fight against corruption in a police department. Then, you would be born into a police family. Your dad is a policemen, your grandpa was a policeman, all your uncles are policemen. And your Path would be to bring this corruption to light. This is not going to be easy

because you live with all these people and so a lot of times you are knocked off your Path because you are swayed by family and friends.

We have "Special Op Angels" who help you. And one sat down with you before you came down here and asked ~ "Shirley, what do you want to do on earth? What are your goals? What do you want to achieve in this human life?" And you replied: "This is what I want to do". And then the Angels find you the appropriate family to come to ~ and so you choose your parents and choose your life. Your parents could be a very rich couple or it could be a single mom who is as poor as a church mouse ~ whatever is necessary for what you want to accomplish. The Angels set you in motion so that you can achieve your goals and you will be put on a Path.

Your Path is not so much about small specific details. It's not that you specifically wanted to meet your husband at a specific time or you specifically wanted to have your children at a specific time. None of that is what we talk about ~ it's never that detailed ~ those are enhancements to your life and they simply come to you. Your kids come to you. Your son chose you,

your daughter chose you and you are an instrument for each other to use to get to where they want to go in their Path and you in yours. You only have your children a short time in your life and they need to do what they need to do because they have a Mission here as well. You have a Mission here, Colleen has a Mission here ~ everyone has a Mission here ~ which you call your 'Journey'. It's up to your specific Guardian Angel to help you stay on the Path of your Journey. And there are many, many things that you're supposed to experience in your life, both big and small. Wonderful things and sorrowful things that you are supposed to experience ~ but these are things you *wanted* to experience.

Wonderful things would be having a child, smelling a flower, having good friends, laughing. Sorrowful things would be having a child die, seeing someone in pain, seeing somebody become an addict. If your goal, your Path, is to be empathetic ~ to have more empathy towards other people ~ you need to have things happen to you so that you then can empathize with other people. Other people will accept your

comfort and advice more whole-heartedly, if you can identify with their situation and their feelings.

Human beings are not privy to their Path. You have a Mission and enhancements come to you along your Journey, but it would be impossible for a human being "to go with the flow" if you knew your Path. Only your Guardian Angel knows your Path. They know who you're supposed to meet. They know where you're suppose to live. If you're supposed to go to college and what college you're supposed to go to. They know all of these details because these put you in touch with people you are supposed to meet and help along the way. A person cannot ask, "What is my Path?" But, if they tune into their heart, every person who is not on their Path can tell immediately that they are off their Path because they don't feel right in their heart and things may be spiraling down hill.

More than half the humans who walk the earth right now are here to see how it's like to live differently from a previous life. When a Spirit returns to the Light, they immediately know what their Path was and how far off that Path they went and it upsets them. So over time they want to come back to make

amends. I would call that doing 'penance' and penance is their Path ~ to undo everything that they did wrong in a past life. For every action, word, or thought that they committed that was not of a "light and love" nature, most Spirits feel sorry or remorseful and will ask for forgiveness and will do penance. Penance is to think or say or do the opposite of what you originally did or said or thought. It could have been 700 years ago and they are just now coming back to earth. It took them that long to get themselves ready to be able to do this because it takes a very strong Spirit to choose to make amends. The person who comes down to earth to do penance has a very strong Spirit. God is never going to allow you to come back if you're weak. You have to have a very strong Spirit because sometimes you have to fight your whole life against people who oppose you, even people who are close to you, such as family members.

Some Spirits come down to help others, and along the way they learn about themselves. You usually don't come back to somebody in the life you just left, such as a child or a grandchild in the same family. When you come to earth, you don't remember your

past lives and so you don't have a connection with anybody. But all humans are connected to humans simply because they are human. We are all God's children. A lot of Spirits come to help a person by giving unconditional love. A child may come into the lives of two parents and because the baby accepts them, it may allow the parents to accept themselves and perhaps realize that they were not living their truth and raising this child is what they need to do. Helping out others has all to do with love and acceptance ~ towards everyone. You cannot have enough friends ~ enough people who love you or whom you love ~ there's no such thing.

You are human and to be human means to care about yourself and to care about everybody else and to help one another. The only way you can truly be happy is by helping people ~ and not just helping people you know. There are a lot of people who help their own, but would never think of helping a stranger. They're missing out on so much of their humanness. You can never find out who you are until you can totally shed your shortsightedness and help other people regardless whether you know them

or not. It's like wearing the heaviest winter coat in 95-degree temperature while running a 25-mile race. You have to shed that off in order to be in the running and to be of help. There are no class distinctions when you're at the Light. There is no such thing as being in a clique, which many on earth are in. If everybody helped everybody else, we wouldn't have any of the problems that we have right now ~ none of them ~ they would all go away. If everyone loved themselves and accepted themselves, there would be no prejudices because everyone would have the same total acceptance of others as they have of themselves.

Many people lose their way and get off their Path. It's never on your Path to kill people. It's never on your Path to rape people or do physical harm to somebody. It is never on your Path to be a bully. Someone may come down here because their father is a bully and there are two older siblings who are both bullies and they come to change that and instead, what happens, is that their family changes them and they become a bully. You don't purposely set yourself up to come to earth to be a bully, or a rapist, or a murderer, or a terrorist ~ you don't come to

experience that. You have a different Path, but along
the way things happen to you and you get messed
up and there you are terrorizing kids in school or in
the neighborhood. And then when you get older,
you wind up being a manager somewhere and you
terrorize everybody who comes near you because you
feel entitled to be able to do that because this is the
way you were raised. And even though you originally
came down here to deflect all that ~ to show kindness
and love and teach people that this is not the way
to live ~ you end up off your Path. This is not what
always happens, but it can. However, a lot of times,
instead, things work out right and you do change
their hearts.

Another scenario may be that you have a father or
mother who is very prejudiced against a certain race
of people. And you get a little older and you're a
female and you get pregnant by someone from that
same race. And all of a sudden your parents now
have a grandchild or a niece or nephew who is of
the race they ridiculed and hated. And now all of
a sudden that's their blood pumping through the
veins of that baby. You had to give those prejudiced

parents a grandchild or a niece or nephew or a great grandchild for them to accept that race of people. You wouldn't believe how many people have hated their whole life ~ until all of a sudden they are close to someone who gets pregnant by someone of the race they hated.

Or, maybe their daughter or granddaughter is a lesbian and she's with a female partner and they adopt a baby. Then all of sudden the parents or grandparents are in a situation that they hated because their daughter or granddaughter is involved with another woman ~ but they love the baby and accept the situation to be around the baby. That's how you bring them around. It's actually love that is allowing them to see through their prejudices. And so many of them may have been hateful a long time but you were able to change their hearts.

When you start bucking your Path, that's when problems come and bad things start happening. You're at your worst when you start piling too many things on your plate and things get overwhelming. There are so many people out there who think they can handle all that ~ but they can't ~ they think they're coping ~

but it's too much. They're juggling 96 balls in the air at a time and then they drop a few. But what if the ball they are dropping is one of their kids? Their child then is not getting something from the mom or dad that they are suppose to be getting because they're juggling too many balls, and they can't.

You need to clear your plate of all the complications that life has brought you. Keep it simple, find the beauty in everything and simply do what's right in front of you. Above all, people need to get in touch with their heart. Feel that intuitive feeling that comes from your heart.

Certainly you have had disappointments in your life ~ there are things that you would have liked to change in your life ~ but most of the things you would not because you would not be who you are today. And this Journey that all humans are on begins the day you take your first breath and it ends the day you take your last breath. And all that time in the middle ~ be it 2 seconds or 120 years ~ that's the Journey that you're on.

What happens when I die?

When you die, for a brief second you are in the dark and all you can see is a portal of light. Let's say you die during your sleep tonight and all of a sudden you wake up and there's a bright light. You will see two people from your past ~ either from this past life or five lifetimes ago ~ it doesn't matter how long ago ~ these are people whom you trusted and loved very much. They are not necessarily a father or mother from the same lifetime or related or even know each other ~ but again, they are two people whom you trust and love. They are beckoning you to come Home through the Light and you have the choice to go or not. The way it's supposed to work is that you just walk through the portal into the Light and you go Home to your loved ones and the Angels will be there to help you understand what is happening to you.

Returning to the Light *is a choice* and not everybody chooses to return to the Light. The people who go immediately to the Light are free to move around and free to look everybody up in the Spirit world ~ your husband, your wife, your friends. You remember all your past lives and want to see if Spirits who you

know are at the Light now, because you don't know if they are until you are there yourself.

Once you know that you have died, you have an examination of conscience ~ that's true for everybody. Your conscience reviews the choices you made throughout your life and you realize the rightness or wrongness of your behavior. And this takes place in a split second ~ you know how long a second is ~ literally a split second. You remember all the things you did to people, said to people, whether you harmed people or harmed yourself with food or drugs ~ any of those things. And the thing is, it's not only what you did, but also what you *didn't do* in your lifetime that matters. And the more important one is what you *didn't do*. It's all the opportunities when you could have said something nice or comforting to somebody. You could have told somebody that you forgave them. You could have told somebody that you loved them.

Through the Light is Home. And in that moment when you pass ~ you will then realize what your Path was to be ~ who you were suppose to be with and the things that you were supposed to accomplish and then

you decide. You decide whether you're going to stay in the darkness or whether you're going to go through the portal into the Light. *It's always your choice.* You can stay in the darkness ~ which is the dimension between earth and the Light ~ but the Light will always be there for you to enter. Even if you think you are turning your back against it, the Light is always there and you will always see it. The two beloved and trusted people are still beckoning you with open arms and at any time you can decide to walk through the portal into the Light. But, sometimes people are afraid and fear is a big driving factor for staying in the dark.

Again, in your life review after death, it's the things you *didn't do* ~ the things you didn't say ~ the people you didn't help when you could have ~ that matter. And we're not talking about people in other countries that you have not met. We're talking about people in your own lifetime ~ in your own circle ~ people who needed you. People whom you knew were hurting ~ whom you heard about from other people. You could have called them and said, "How are you doing? I was thinking about you today." The response could

be, "I really needed to hear from you today". And these are the things that make you the happiest. *It's the small things that we do that matter.*

A person may feel, "I should have done this or that" or "I should have been kinder to people" or "I shouldn't have been critical of people ~ should have helped people and should have loved more and I didn't do any of that". When you're standing all alone and you're in the dark looking into the Light, there's no denying that it was *your* life and these were *your* decisions. They were the choices you made and you know right away whether they were good or bad. You may decide that you're not ready to go into the Light because you really messed up and think they're going to be really mad at you, so you decide not to go Home and stay in the darkness.

But, nobody judges you ~ God doesn't judge you ~ he created you and he wants you Home with him.

There are those who have died and are standing before the Light who come to the realization that they have passed but want to stay on earth with somebody ~ maybe they have a handicapped child or a husband

who won't survive without them ~ and feel they need to stay with them and be with them. That's never a good choice for that Spirit and it's a worse decision for the person whom they're staying to help because they actually do the opposite of that. The person the Spirit chooses to stay with has their own agenda ~ their Path ~ which conflicts with that of the deceased Spirit. Trying to help by staying with someone never works out because the deceased Spirit is in the dark and the living person is trying to be helped by a being in the dark, not a being in the Light.

Another reason for someone not going to the Light when they die would be when someone on earth grieves so hard for the death of their loved one that they hold them back in the dark. It could be a child who doesn't want a twin sister or a mother to go or a parent who doesn't want their child to go and they grieve so hard that they hold back the Spirit. But again the situation is the same: it's never a good choice for the human to do that and it's a worse choice for the Spirit because they want to go on to the Light and this person's holding them back. This is why

it's critical to go Home *immediately* ~ so that someone doesn't hold you back.

Those are the reasons why at the moment of death ~ when you're standing in the darkness deciding whether to go through the Light or not ~ some Spirits stay in the darkness. Speed is everything: the second you die ~ the next second you should be walking through the portal of light and going Home.

If more time goes on and you linger in the dark, there can be different people beckoning you to come to the Light and this can be confusing. Let's say you've been dead 30 years and you now see a child who outlived you who is now a Spirit in the Light beckoning you to come Home. You left the earth when this child was 30 years younger and living a nice life and you can't understand why you see them at the Light because they were alive when you died.

There are many people who die suddenly and don't realize that they died. You could drop dead all of a sudden or somebody shoots you or you get in a car accident. You can see what's happening around you. You're still in your body and you can see anybody

who comes to look at you but they can't hear you and you're trying to tell them that you're not dead by using body language. When you don't think you're dead, you're going to fight everything. "Well, I can't be dead! ~ I have a lot to do! ~ Christmas is coming and family is coming over and I've got shopping to do ~ all of these things ~ I can't be dead!" So they resist the Spirits who are beckoning them from the Light.

Many people are taken sooner then they were suppose to and didn't complete their Path and they know that when they get to the Light. They know they were suppose to have more years on earth. For example, a daughter who was going to help her mother and then all of a sudden she's coming home from work and got killed in a car accident by a drunk driver. She thinks, "I died and I needed to help my mother and I didn't do that". She didn't complete her Mission even though she didn't know this when she was alive because her mother wasn't sick yet. She thinks about how she needs to be there for her but her mother hadn't even started on that part of her Path yet and now she is gone. But this kind of thinking should still not keep you from going immediately into the Light.

Many didn't have time to make amends for the things that they did ~ they bullied people or hurt them in other ways or they stole or cheated or whatever. But when you die your conscience does not die. Instead, it comes fully awake so that there is no hiding from it. You know immediately if you did bad things. I don't care what you told yourself for the last 15 years of your life ~ you can't talk fast enough when you're dead to convince yourself in that state when you're between the earth and the Light that it was okay to do bad things. You know that's not an okay thing to do and you've always known that. You convinced yourself while on earth, that it was okay because everybody did it. And now you know it's not okay: "Oh my God, what did I do? No, it wasn't okay. But I let myself be deceived and how stupid that was!" They think the Light is not a good place to be because they really messed up, so they choose not to go.

They may feel they're unworthy ~ "I'm a bad person!" and "God's going to be mad at me!". God's not going to mad at you. What you need to do at the end of your life is just go Home ~ all is forgiven. It's *you* who has to forgive *yourself.* God has already forgiven

you ~ there's nothing for him to forgive. It was your choice ~ he didn't make you do anything ~ he didn't tell you to do this or do that.

It is your choice ~ you need to love yourself and forgive yourself and go Home.

If you commit suicide, the second you pass, you know immediately that this is something that you should not have done. Like people who die naturally, the moment you pass, you will see the portal of light and two people beckoning you Home and the next second you should be walking through that portal ~ but that will take a long long time if you take your own life. You realize that you should have listened to your Angel. Whether you knew you had an Angel or not when you were living ~ you certainly know you have an Angel now. You know immediately that there was hope there but you were so depressed and so enthralled with all the negative things in your life. You should have asked for help. There were people out there who could have helped you. But you felt isolated and alone and hated yourself and thought that nobody could love you ~ so you just never reached out to anybody. And if you refused help or

refused to ask somebody for help ~ this is all as much on your mind when you pass as everything else.

What is needed is for you to forgive yourself. That's always the thing you need to do. Humans who committed suicide don't want to go to the Light because they're afraid. But they must forgive themselves or it's just not going to happen and they will stay in the darkness. All Spirits belong in the Light and everybody should go Home.

The experience of being in the darkness can be compared to the pain of not knowing where a loved one is or of wanting desperately to be with someone who is missing. People with missing loved ones want to know what has happened to them because it's the not knowing that is so painful ~ that's the most pain a human can have. That's how Spirits feel when they don't go to the Light ~ it is the pain of knowing that they're not Home ~ it's suffocating. It's like the feeling of a parent or grandparent who suddenly has a missing child. As if you are in a store talking to your daughter or granddaughter and you turn around for a second and she's gone and you can't see her. You're calling her name and get no response when just a few

seconds ago she was right there. Then minutes go on and you still can't find her. You have a sense of confusion and panic: that's what a lot of people feel when they pass and don't go immediately to the Light.

If you've been laying in a coma for a month or a year and you're waiting to die and you haven't yet forgiven yourself ~ you still have that feeling. You're in the dark and you're lost and you're trying to find somebody and you can't find them. If you still were in your body, a heaviness would overcome you and it would feel like a vise on your whole entire body. You are in a state of fear and you don't want to stay in that state of fear. But it will immediately go away once you forgive yourself, choose to go Home and you walk through that portal of light into the arms of your loved ones who are waiting for you.

Those who take awhile to get to the Light ~ the ones who stay in that interim place of darkness ~ when they do go to the Light they go to an encampment. Archangel Uriel heads the encampment for these Spirits who had a hard time getting to the Light. She wants to make sure that they are in good shape before putting them in the mix with all the other Spirits.

In this encampment there are loving Angels to help them figure things out, so that they can arrive at a state of peace with themselves. There is a lot of sorrow in those encampments because a lot of the recently departed Spirits never got a chance to fulfill their Path because they were abruptly taken off the earth, and the Spirits who had a hard time forgiving themselves, come with remorseful feelings. The Angels hear a lot of regret and sorrow from Spirits in the encampment.

The encampment Spirits are having a hard time adjusting to death and feel sorrow for a Path not fulfilled and may have regrets for actions done or not done in their life. It's like a rehabilitation hospital ~ but the Angels call it an encampment ~ and there's nothing but love and forgiveness there. The Angels there are trying to get you the Spirit to forgive yourself for the things you didn't do. God wants you to be happy and the only way you can be happy is if you love yourself. In the encampments all of that love and all of that understanding heal the suffering Spirits. Archangel Uriel is the one who discharges you when

you are ready and then you can go into the main gathering of Spirits and move around freely.

People need to forgive themselves and say "I'll do better next time" and go into the Light.

Love yourself ~ love yourself here on earth ~ so that when you pass ~ the moment that you die ~ there's not going to be a time lapse during which you're going to say "Oh my God, I did the wrong thing!" ~ and stay in that darkness. If you love yourself in life and know that you did everything you could to help people ~ nobody's perfect ~ but you know that you did more good than bad ~ you'll be fine. There is euphoria at the Light and that's the best part of being a Spirit at the Light!

What about animals?

When God created the earth, first he put flowers,
trees and plants ~ living things to beautify the
planet ~ and they were here millions of years before
animals. And then God put animals on this earth
and they lived for centuries before mankind came.
They learned to live in harmony with each another
and respect one another and take care of one another
regardless whether they were the same type of animal.
God put food on the earth for the animals and they
knew which ones to eat ~ which were good and
sustaining and which ones to stay away from. God
then created human beings and put them on the earth
and the animals and human beings lived on earth
together.

From the beginning animals did not intertwine with
mankind. It's not as if from the very beginning
humans had dogs and cats and birds as family pets
~ those animals were out there, but they really didn't
become companions to mankind. People back then
who lived in caves may have had special animals
around them. Maybe a special bird that would fly
around them and as a child you would name that
bird and they would constantly be around you until it

passed or you passed. As time went on, God saw to
it that some of the animals ~ like dogs, cats, horses ~
got closer to humans and they became companions
to them.

Animals are also tools for mankind and help people
all the time. There are many domesticated animals
that help people ~ mostly dogs ~ such as seeing eye
dogs for the blind, or dogs trained to help soldiers
coming home with disabilities. Other animals can
also help human beings. There are many people who
just love to sit in a park and watch the birds, watch
butterflies fly by or watch the squirrels play. People
go into the jungle and watch from a distance the
water buffalo, elephants and giraffes, just to see these
creatures of nature in their own environment.

There are hundreds of millions of people on this
earth who think much more of animals than they do
of human beings. They spend billions of dollars on
food, medicines, trinkets and clothes to dress up their
animals because they adore them. They adore them
because animals don't care if you're having a bad hair
day or what you look like or what you say, as long as
it's positive and loving, that's all they care about. And

human beings all need to treat one another like most people treat their animals ~ in a good, loving way.

Human beings cannot come back to earth as animals because you have a Spirit and animals do not have a Spirit ~ they have an "Essence" ~ which is not the same as a Spirit. Animals are pure love because Essence is pure love. Dogs always come back as dogs, cats as cats, horses as horses.

You never choose your pet ~ they choose you ~ because they know instinctively when they are born who they need to go to. They will try to get to you whether you go to a place to pick out a puppy or whether they show up to your door. They are choosing you ~ you're the one they came here for. They are here on earth for you. This applies to all domestic pets. An animal's Essence can come back down into the same lifetime of a human, if the Essence is still needed. An Essence may also come back to a Spirit over several lifetimes if the Spirit is having the same needs that brought the Essence to them in the first place.

God has given all living beings ~ including animals ~ the choice to return to the Light. And when they die they also will have an examination of conscience and they will go through a review of their life and most animals will go back through the Light. If an animal was sick or had distemper or rabies or was beaten ~ that can mess up their brains. They don't want to do these bad things but they lash out and bite. And so some of them, when they die, think, "Well, I hurt people or other animals and I didn't want to do that". So, some of them don't go through the Light because it's their choice to stay behind. But we're talking here about maybe only 1 out of 50,000 animals, a really small number if you compare it to the number of Spirits who don't return Home right away once they die ~ way more animals go right to the Light after death than do Spirits.

Most people who have animals know that animals have hearts and that they love and they can be sad or disappointed when you leave them alone. Sometimes they act out when they're left alone because they miss you and they want you to be around all the time. Animals can hurt and bleed ~ they can be broken,

beaten, hit by a car and they can get sick. Any kind
of disease that humans can get they can get ~ cancer,
colds ~ any of those things.

*Animals were put on the earth by God and they
should be respected and loved as you should respect
and love yourself.*

What can I do
to lead a better life?

Every single human being knows what they personally need to do to lead a better life or to improve their life. The first thing is to love yourself and the second thing is to accept yourself ~ then everything falls into place like a domino effect. To love yourself is to forgive yourself, forgive others, give yourself a break, give others a break, love yourself and love others. But you also have to work on your faults, and try everyday to change what you see as a stumbling block in front of you. Believe me, if you work on yourself, you will have no time to look at others and compare, judge or criticize them.

First and foremost ~ love yourself. If you love yourself ~ everything else falls into place ~ every problem you've ever had. Loving yourself is accepting yourself for who you are and who you have become and what you do. What you do, then goes forward. And you pay everything forward by encouraging people who are in your life. Suppose you're at a store and standing in line to pay and overhear a conversation, make an encouraging comment on it and say, for instance, "That was a good job!". You don't have to carry on a huge conversation

with somebody ~ just smile at people ~ do positive things!

If you loved yourself ~ if everybody loved themselves ~ there would be no hatred on earth. Nobody would hate anybody because you would be accepting of and loving towards everybody. You're all different, certainly you don't look alike, you're not the same size or height or have the same body frame or the same color eyes or the same color hair. You don't live in the same house or have the same parents. Humans are a very diverse society of people and that is what makes them all special and should make them all wonderful. Diversity is what you should be most proud of and you should celebrate your differences ~ but you need to be accepting of yourself first and then you will accept everybody else.

And you could sit here and ask me about yourself: "What if?, What if?, What if?, What about this?, What about that?" Behind all of these questions is the same thing ~ you are judging yourself. And because you judge yourself, then you're going to judge everybody else. Quit judging yourself and then you won't judge others and all these "What if's" will go away. You're

going to live a good life and the best thing about your life is that people are going to want to be around you. Not just people in your family and circle of friends ~ all mankind will want to be around you. It's like the Gandhi syndrome. Mahatma Gandhi was so good ~ people called him "holy" ~ people called him "gifted" ~ people called him "enlightened". Gandhi lived a simple life and because he loved himself, he never judged anybody.

Many people think ~ "An eye for an eye and a tooth for a tooth" ~ that's just ridiculous to think that way ~ and it never, never, never works out! That's why the best people do not think this way. Nelson Mandela is a good example. The first question that the world wanted to ask when Mandela was released from prison was, "How are you going to get back at those people who imprisoned you for 27 years?" And the first words out of his mouth were: "I'm going to forgive them and let it go ~ I gave them 27 years and I'm not giving them a second more". And he went on with his life and he made something of his life and that is why he was so beloved by millions in the world. Mandela did not turn around and gather up

an army to start another war, which is exactly what they did not need over there.

It is hard to forgive people who have done you harm and then move on with your life. They don't need to be your best friend ~ but you cannot let that hatred rule your life ~ and it will. You will get so consumed with the hate and the negative energy of trying to find a way to get back at them. That's the same with kids in school who fight back and forth, using all kinds of electronics to do hurtful, hateful things to other kids. Then, those kids try to get back at the others and it never ends up good and nobody ever gets anywhere.

It's not necessarily only among children, that's in a workplace also ~ it's all over the place. People need to speak up! For example, let's say there's 500 people who work in the same building and one of them is spreading false rumors about a co-worker. If no one steps up to the person spreading the rumor and says: "Shame on you! This is wrong to do!", then he will simply go on thinking that the other 499 people in the building believe that he is in the right in spreading the rumors. Nobody's telling him it's wrong ~ so they are

just as bad as he is ~ he thinks that you agree with him because you're not saying anything.

People are afraid to get involved and it's now, more then ever that people need to get involved. There is a kind of "silent majority" of good people out there who don't let their voices be heard. So all you hear are negative things, bad things that a few people are spreading around. And because the "silent majority" sits back and says ~ "Well they just don't get it ~ so what? ~ I'm not going to say anything even though they are totally wrong" ~ these evil-doers get away with it. Unfortunately, people are becoming more and more arrogant in their evil and saying ~ "Everybody feels this way". "Shirley feels this way". "Colleen feels this way". But you don't feel this way. Yet, if you don't speak up and say "No I don't feel that way!" ~ who's going to know that you don't ~ nobody's going to know.

Stand up and be counted when wrongs are being done. Right now, one of the biggest problems on earth is that people don't speak up! The time of the "silent majority" needs to end. People need to speak up when they hear things that they don't agree with on a

spiritual or moral level ~ or just even on the level
of information or knowledge, when ignorant people
are spreading misinformation.

All this negativity would go away if good people
stepped forward. Bad people wouldn't be able to
move ~ everybody would surround them ~ it would
be 6,000 people deep and the bad people wouldn't
be able to go anywhere. They would be shamed into
doing the right thing. Recall the old adage ~ "It takes
a village to raise an infant"~ well, humanity is your
village and this is the village you joined. It's called
humanity because you're on earth and everybody
needs to join together to help people ~ to truly help
people ~ that's how you grow spiritually. *Helping
people is a present to yourself!*

And one of the biggest ways to help others is by
simply *listening* to them. That's the biggest gift that
any human can give to any other human ~ to just
listen to them. That's what people want most of all.
They don't want a hand out, even though they think
they do or you might think they do. They just want
to be listened to. But you also have to empathize with
them, and hug them and hold their hand and let them

know that you're there for them. They don't want you to say, "Well, this is what I would do" or "This is what you should say". They just want somebody to listen to them. You don't have to say you understand unless you just went through their thing. That, more likely than not, will give them the courage to keep on trying to do whatever it is they need to do. They're using you as a sounding board ~ they're not looking for advice.

Another big thing that mankind needs to learn ~ that it has totally forgot about ~ and I mean totally, totally forgot about ~ is "tolerance"! The first person whom humans are not tolerant of are themselves and because they are not tolerant of themselves, they're not tolerant of anybody. If you do not have tolerance for yourself, you cannot have tolerance for anybody else. That is something that you cannot fake even though you think you can. It's just like love ~ if you don't love yourself, you cannot love anyone else. You can't, because you don't know what it is. It's like carrying around a fancy 17-letter word that you don't know how to pronounce and you don't know what it means ~ but you think you can sell this bill of goods ~

this 17-letter word ~ to everyone else on earth and you don't even know what it is.

If you don't have tolerance and love for yourself and accept yourself no matter what ~ then you can't accept others. And absolutely everybody makes choices that they're not really proud of, whether they are about trivial things or really big things. This is how you learn ~ by making mistakes ~ this is how you grow and this is how you forgive yourself.

Everybody needs to take care of their own self first. You need to be loving of yourself, forgiving of yourself, tolerant of yourself and then you can be a giving human being. This is what God created ~ this is what mankind is all about ~ it's that basic. There are millions of people who walk this earth right now who are so far from that. It's as basic as the fact that you need air to breathe. You can't stick your head in water and expect to survive very long. You are a human being and you need air and you need food and you need water and you also need acceptance of yourself. You need love ~ you cannot expect anybody to love you if you don't love yourself. These are the big things mankind is lacking.

The earth can and should be a great place to live, but along the way people strayed from their God-given true nature and bad things began to happen. The vast majority of people are very, very good ~ there are relatively very few negative people. For every 10,000 people, there are only two who are murdering, stealing and doing others harm. There are millions of good people who walk this earth and who love themselves and don't judge others.

Bullies will call these good people weak and they are prey for the bullies on this earth. What the bullies don't know is that they are at the bottom of the heap and they're trying to claw themselves from the bottom and get above everybody. But, they can't because people are not going to put up with that anymore. And when the bullies make excuses and claim "It's not my fault" ~ "My mom did this to me" ~ "My dad did that to me" ~ "I had a teacher who berated me" ~ "It's not my fault" ~ "I'm this way because of somebody else" ~ that's all bunk. You are the way you are because you choose to be that way ~ always ~ that's the short and long of it, period.

The best thing that every human being can do towards creating a better life for themselves, is to take a deep breath and go where the universe is leading you ~ go with the flow. You'll find that your life is so much easier. And it's not that all your problems will be solved, but you will suffer less ~ it's just so much easier ~ you understand more and you will never be any happier than you are at that moment. Let it be the philosophy of your entire life ~ not just a few moments in your life ~ *go with the flow*. If you feel that nature is guiding you somewhere and you've got a gut feeling about it ~ everybody has this ~ follow it.

Listen to your heart!

Many people don't stop to think long enough to connect with their inner self. Is this the right thing for me to do or is this the wrong thing for me to do? If you know deep down in your heart it's the wrong thing ~ don't do it!

Zeduo's Concluding Words

There are bad things going on right now on earth and I am a Guardian Angel and I want to make a difference. I, Zeduo, want to make a difference on earth through the human charges who are in my care. Colleen happens to be the only one I have right now because of the Mission that has been given to her. She was selected for this Mission but had the choice whether to accept it or not. And there was nobody more afraid than she was when she first started channeling: "Why me?" ~ "Why pick me"? Colleen is just a simple woman and that is exactly the type of person I needed and wanted. Somebody completely believable, not pretentious at all, who doesn't come from money and is kind and gentle.

The facts in the book that you're reading right now ~ *this is what it is.* If you can't love yourself ~ nobody on earth is going to love you ~ because you can't love yourself. If you can't forgive yourself, then nobody's going to forgive you. That's just how it works. We're not here to make people believe anything. We're here to just state the facts. *This is it ~ this is what it is.* This is God's truth. God loves you and you belong Home with God.

When your life ends, you need to go Home. When you pass and see the portal of light and people you love ~ forgive yourself and go immediately to their open arms. This is what this is all about.

Keep your life simple, love yourself, forgive yourself ~ be kind and loving to all living things.

~ Zeduo

www.ingramcontent.com/pod-product-compliance
Lightning Source LLC
Chambersburg PA
CBHW061733020426
42331CB00006B/1228